16560

298
394.2683
CHA

A WORLD OF FESTIVALS

ALL SAINTS
ALL SOULS
AND HALLOWE'EN

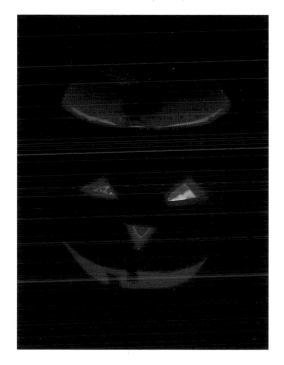

Catherine Chambers

Evans Brothers Limited

D0319490

Published by Evans Brothers Limited
2A Portman Mansions
Chiltern Street
London W1M 1LE

© copyright Evans Brothers Limited 1997

All Rights Reserved. No part of this publication may
be reproduced, stored in a retrieval system or
transmitted in any form, or by any means, electronic,
mechanical, photocopying, recording or otherwise,
without prior permission of Evans Brothers Limited.

British Library Cataloguing in Publication data.
A catalogue record for this book is available from the
British Library.

First published 1997
Reprinted 1997
Printed in Spain by G.Z. Printek

0 237 51695 0

16560

AYLESBURY COLLEGE   298
                      394   2683
LIBRARY   CHA

ACKNOWLEDGEMENTS

Editor: Su Swallow
Design: Neil Sayer
Production: Jenny Mulvanny

For permission to reproduce copyright material, the
author and publishers gratefully acknowledge the fol-
lowing:

Cover Hutchison Library
Title page Emma Lee/Life File
page 5 Robert Harding Picture Library **page 6**
Edward Parker/Hutchison Library **page 7** (top left)
Last Resort (bottom right) Hutchison Library **page 8**
David Reed/Panos Pictures **page 9** (top) Ronald
Sheridan/Ancient Art and Architecture Collection
(bottom) Hutchison Library **page 10** (top) Robert
Francis/Hutchison Library (bottom) Mike Potter/Life
File **page 11** Sally-Anne Fison/Life File **page 12** (top)
Jeremy Hartley/Panos Pictures (bottom) David
Cumming/Eye Ubiquitous **page 13** Billie Cook/Life
File **page 14** (top) Crispin Hughes/Panos Pictures
(bottom) Trevor Page/Hutchison Library **page 15**
(top) James Davis Travel Photography (bottom)
Robert Francis/Hutchison Library **page 16** Circa
Photo Library/John Smith **page 17** (top) Ancient Art
and Architecture Collection (bottom) James Davis
Travel Photography **page 18** Collections/Brian Shuel
page 19 (top) Emma Lee/Life File (bottom) Gregory
Wrona/Panos Pictures **page 20** Simon Arnold/Eye
Ubiquitous **page 21** (top) Robert Frerck/Robert
Harding Picture Library (bottom) Andy Purcell/Bruce
Coleman Limited **page 22** (top) Robert
Frerck/Robert Harding Picture Library (bottom)
Robert Francis/Hutchison Library **page 23** Alan
Towse Photography **page 24** George McCarthy/Bruce
Coleman Limited **page 25** (top) Angela Maynard/Life
File (bottom) Robert Harding Picture Library **page
26** Frank Lane Picture Agency **page 27** Mary Evans
Picture Library **page 28** Alan Towse Photography
page 29 Alan Towse Photography

❤ Contents ❤

Spirits, saints and the sun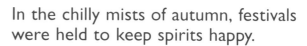

I T IS THE END OF AUTUMN. As winter darkness looms, the souls of the dead and the spirits of kind saints are all remembered with three festivals.

WHEN CAN WE CELEBRATE?

Hallowe'en, All Saints' Day and All Souls' Day bring fire and mystery to the beginning of winter. Together, the three festival days are known as Hallowmas. They are celebrated on October 31st, November 1st and November 2nd. And what a mixture of old and new, good and bad, laughter and sadness they are, too!

In the chilly mists of autumn, festivals were held to keep spirits happy.

CHRISTIANS JOIN IN!

The Christian religion began about 2000 years ago. Christians follow the teachings of Jesus Christ. But long ago, many Christians still wanted to keep their old religious festivals. So the early Church just added their own to the old ones. Their celebrations for the spirits of saints and the souls of the dead fit in well at this time of the year.

At Hallowmas, glowing fires welcomed home the spirits of the dead.

Early November in much of Europe is chilly and misty - a bit spooky, really. Long ago, it was part of people's religion to remember spirits at this time. The good spirits were kept happy with food and warm fires. But the bad ones had to be chased away.

Another religious custom was in honour of the sun. Winter can be a dark time and in those days only lamps and firelight brightened the long nights. It seemed as if the sun would never shine brightly again. So huge fires were lit to give the sun strength through the long winter.

Hallowmas is a time for remembering the spirits of saints. This is Saint Celia, the saint for musicians.

The souls of the dead

PEOPLE FROM ALL OVER THE WORLD believe that the dead have souls that live on. Their spirits can be very powerful - perhaps especially at Hallowe'en and All Souls!

Spirits are important in Africa and the Americas. Healers use these medicines and the power of spirits to cure the sick.

FAMILY SPIRITS

Before the Christian religion burst into northern Africa and Europe, most people believed in many gods - often with one chief god in charge. They also believed in the power of spirits, both good and bad.

Hallowe'en was a very old Anglo-Saxon and Celtic spirit festival - and the beginning of the Celtic New Year.

The Celtic celebration was known as Samhain in those days. Samhain was the Celtic Lord of the Dead. At the festival each family remembered all its ancestors' spirits. The family made new links with them for the year ahead to keep the souls happy.

Samhain judged all the dead souls during the festival. People offered gifts to him. Then he might judge the spirits kindly and let them go home for the night.

But Samhain was a night of turmoil as well. Ghosts and demons rose from the dead and ran around making mischief!

SPIRITS OF THE WORLD

Christians believe in spirits too. They believe in life after death. So it wasn't difficult for the early Church to accept a festival for dead souls.

When people from Europe moved to America about 500 years ago, they took Hallowe'en customs with them. African slaves in America added their own spirit traditions to the Celtic and Christian ones. What a rich mixture!

Some Celtic traditions – and some Celtic jewellery – have survived to today.

In Brazil, Umbanda is one of the most popular African-American spirit religions.

 It's Hallowe'en!

It's October 31st. The spirits of the dead are whirling around in a frenzy! They are trying to find their way home. Witches and demons are on the loose - watch out!

PRAYERS FOR SOULS

The name 'Hallowe'en' was given to this festival by the early Roman Catholic Church. It means 'All Hallows' Eve' - the night before All Saints' Day.

Although Hallowe'en is a really old festival, it's still very much alive.

A woman leaves flowers at a grave in a small Italian town.

In Europe and South America, many people celebrate Hallowe'en with Christian customs.

In the past, people visited the graves of their ancestors. There, they could think about them and say prayers for them. Nowadays, many people still visit graves with candles and greetings cards.

MODERN MISCHIEF

The Celts kept the spirits happy with fires, feasts, dancing and gifts. Some people wore ghostly masks. This was to trick naughty spirits into thinking that the masked people

In a Russian church, a candle is lit for a loved soul.

were spirits too. The people in disguise then, led the wicked demons to the edge of the village. Here, they could do no harm.

Today, Hallowe'en is still mischief time, especially in America. Young and old alike go out and about in spooky clothes and menacing masks. Some dress as witches or demons. But you could be a cartoon character, or even an astronaut if you like. Anything goes!

Two young girls in Texas are out to scare their friends with these spooky skeleton costumes. They're going 'trick-or-treating' (see pages 22-23).

❤A host of saints❤

AT LEAST ONE CHRISTIAN SAINT is remembered on each day of the year. And on the 1st November, there is a celebration for all the saints. But what makes a saint?

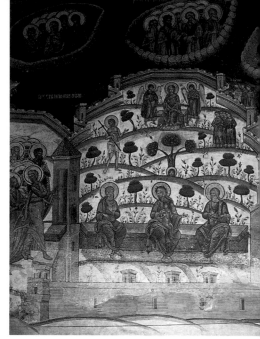

A host of saints in a church in Romania.

It is Saint James' Day in the city of Santiago de Compostela in Spain. The bones of Saint James lie in the church there.

A LONG LIST

Saints became part of the Roman Catholic and Orthodox Churches very early on. At first, all Christians were thought to be saints. But about 100 years later, only people who died for their belief in Jesus Christ became saints. Then the list grew to include Christians who had led good lives. Now there are thousands of them!

Some are the twelve teachers chosen by Jesus Christ. Others are those who helped the sick and the poor. There are lots of special ones, too.

12

Some are the national saints for countries where most people are Christian. For example, Saint James is the saint for Spain. Other saints are special to different kinds of workers, such as fishermen and musicians - or even motorists.

SAINTLY HELP

For many Christians, saints are like real living people. You can pray to a saint in times of trouble. If your life changes for the better, it could be because a saint helped you out. If you want to talk to God, it is sometimes easier to pray to a saint first - and they will talk to God for you. There are lots of festivals for saints. In southern Europe and South America, saints' days are celebrated in a very big way with parades, dancing and fireworks.

Dancing is one of the ways of celebrating saints' days. A maypole is used especially on Saint John's Day here in Spain, and in Portugal too.

All Saints' Day

A service for the saints in the African countryside.

Saints are paraded in the streets on saints' days.

After the spirits and witches of Hallowe'en comes a very different festival. The first day of November is a day for celebrating all the saints - even those who aren't yet born!

SAINTLY STATUES

All Saints' Day is a public holiday in many Roman Catholic countries. There are bells and church services. Statues of the saints are paraded through the streets. But how did this all begin?

THE CHURCH MAKES CHANGES

The early Church wasn't very happy that Christians kept customs linked with witches and bad spirits. But the old traditions would not die. So about 1300 years ago, the Church began to celebrate all the saints instead.

   The first celebration took place when Christian leaders changed the Pantheon of Rome into a church. The Pantheon was a temple full of statues of the old Roman gods. The Christian Church wanted to get rid

This huge church in Rome now remembers all the saints that died for their faith. But it was once known as the Pantheon, a temple for all the Roman gods.

of it. But they wanted to give people something in its place. So they made it into a church for all the saints who had died for their Christian faith.

Then about 200 years later, the Pope, the leader of the Roman Catholic Church, decided to hold a Festival of All Saints at the beginning of November. The Pope knew that this was when the biggest festivals for ancient religions took place in northern Europe.

This was a clever idea. It let people celebrate their old festivals. But it gave them a new Christian one as well.

Greenstead Church in England was built over 1300 years ago by the Saxons. It was one of the first English churches to hold the Festival of All Saints.

✌ All Souls' Day ✌

THE SPIRITS HAVE SETTLED and the witches have flown. Saints in all their glory have been praised. On November 2nd, the souls of the dead must now be properly honoured. Then they too can rest.

PRAYERS FOR THE DEAD

In many churches all over the world, people gather to pray for the dead on All Souls' Day. The Roman Catholic Church holds three full services, or masses, to give peace to their souls. In Mexico, the festival is very special. It is known as the Day of the Dead. But you'd think that after Hallowe'en, people wouldn't want any more festivals for dead souls. So why did the festival of All Souls take place?

After festivals for mischievous spirits and good saints, ordinary souls really needed one of their own. So, nearly 1000 years after the birth of Jesus Christ, the Church gave them a festival of their own. It began in Cluny, in France. Over the next 300 years the festival spread to southern and eastern Europe, and to the British Isles.

THE CRIES OF LOST SOULS

Some people believe that the festival began with a story of a Christian man who made a holy journey all the way to Jerusalem. This was the city where Jesus Christ had died.

On his return, the ship broke up

A Roman Catholic mass is held for the souls of the dead, so that they can rest in peace.

in a stormy sea. The Christian was tossed on to an island. There he met a man who said he could hear the cries of dead souls. They were coming from a crack that went deep into burning rock. The Christian travelled on to the church at Cluny. There, he told his story to the head monk, or abbot, who then made November 2nd a day to pray for all dead souls, to give them peace.

▲ When a Christian was shipwrecked on his way home from Jerusalem he was told about the cries of dead souls.

◄ The French abbey church of Cluny is where the festival of All Souls began.

17

Furious fires and glowing lights

IN NOVEMBER, the Celts lit bonfires to keep the sun burning through the winter. Now, pumpkin lanterns warn off bad spirits. And candles shine for the souls of the dead.

BUILD A BONFIRE!

There's nothing like the smell of an autumn bonfire! Long ago at this time, bonfire ashes were spread over farmland to help crops grow. This custom fitted in well with the fires that warmed the weak winter sun. The Catholic Church didn't mind keeping these traditions at Hallowmas.

But 500 years ago, some European Christians didn't like Catholic customs. These Christians became a separate group called Protestants.

After November 5th, 1605, English Protestants made an autumn fire festival of their own. A Catholic, Guy Fawkes, was killed for trying to blow up the Protestant government on November 5th, which was then made a national holiday. It became a day for burning great bonfires, with dummies of poor Guy Fawkes on top.

In Britain, people still burn poor Guy Fawkes on bonfire night. The 'Guy' is made from old clothes stuffed with newspaper or straw.

A LIGHT FOR EVERY SOUL

On Hallowe'en, Irish people hollowed out turnips and set candles in them. This was to turn away demons, who were afraid of the light. When the Irish came to America, they found that pumpkins made even better lanterns than turnips. That's why we have pumpkin lanterns today.

Cosy fires were lit at Hallowe'en to warm chilly rooms. Then the souls of dead ancestors might come home.

The Christian Church added their own customs. On Hallowe'en Eve, Catholics in Europe and South America carry candles to the graves of each of their loved ones.

▶ Does this pumpkin lantern give you a nice warm feeling - or does it scare you to death?

In a Polish cemetery, masses of candles are lit for the souls of people who have died.

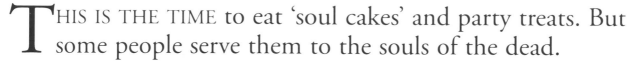

Feeding the living and the dead

THIS IS THE TIME to eat 'soul cakes' and party treats. But some people serve them to the souls of the dead.

COOKING FOR SOULS

Hundreds of years ago, people set out food and wine for their ancestors' spirits, to welcome them home. Later, the Church asked people to bake soul cakes instead. These were given to the poor, who then prayed for the givers' dead ancestors. After many years, boys went from house to house singing songs for the souls. They hoped to get soul cakes or even money in return!

NO TALKING AT TABLE!

Have you ever heard of the 'dumb supper'? This is an eerie Hallowmas meal - no one speaks, not even a whisper. It encourages spirits to come to table. The 'dumb supper' was brought to America by Africans.

THE MEXICAN DAY OF THE DEAD

In Mexico on November 1st, women and young girls carry food to the cemeteries at midnight. They light candles and set up huge statues of skeletons. The men and young boys sing outside the cemetery gates. Inside, the food is offered first to the souls of the ancestors. Then, on November 2nd, as the Day of the Dead dawns, the food is shared out among the people.

Soul cakes in the shape of graves are sold in Mexico City for the Day of the Dead.

20

On the Day of the Dead in Mexico, masses of flowers, glowing lights and gifts show respect for the dead.

NUTCRACKER NIGHT

In Britain, it was thought that the devil was a nut-gatherer. So at Hallowe'en, nuts were used as magic charms. If a girl puts a sprig of rosemary herb and a silver sixpence under her pillow on Hallowe'en night, she will see her future husband in a dream!

Hazelnuts have special magical powers, especially at Hallowe'en.

Gruesome games

Aaaaagh! An American trick-or-treater will frighten the life out of you!

Trick-or-treating and apple-bobbing. These are two of the ghastly and ghostly games played at Hallowe'en.

TRICK OR TREAT? TRICK OR TREAT?

America is the place to go for Hallowe'en fun. Over the last 200 years, the games have become brighter and richer. One of the greatest ways of having fun is to dress up in disguise. You can go to a Hallowe'en party or parade in the street. But children get most fun out of trick-or-treating. The custom is a mixture of old Irish traditions and going round houses singing for soul cakes.

Scary skeletons and spooky spiders' webs decorate a house in New Baltimore in the United States.

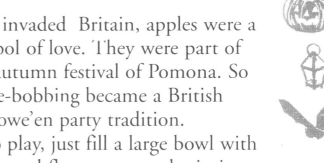

Dressed up as witches, clowns or even Mickey Mouse, children wait till dark. Then they knock on neighbours' doors, shouting 'Trick or treat? Trick or treat?' If you don't want to get a nasty surprise, you'd better give them some sweets or fruit! Many children trick-or-treat to collect money for charity.

HAPPY APPLE-BOBBING!

Apples are magic! Ancient Celts in Britain believed that heaven was filled with apple trees bursting with flowers and fruit. For the Romans, who invaded Britain, apples were a symbol of love. They were part of the autumn festival of Pomona. So apple-bobbing became a British Hallowe'en party tradition.

To play, just fill a large bowl with water and float some apples in it. Ask each party-goer in turn to put their hands behind their back. Then get them to bend over the bowl and try to catch an apple stalk with their teeth. Then they can pull the apple out and eat it. No hands, mind! It isn't as easy as it looks. And you're bound to get your face wet!

These boys are hoping that the girls will drop their apples. No such luck!

Hallowe'en animals

OWLS, BATS, SNAILS AND BLACK CATS. Are they lucky, or just plain spooky? They've been an important part of Hallowe'en for hundreds of years.

FOUL OWLS

'Oh, no! Can you hear that owl hooting? Someone's going to die!' People used to think that owls swooped down to eat the souls of the dying. So if they heard an owl hooting, they were frightened. So what do you do to stop an owl hooting? Try turning your pockets inside out and you'll be alright!

BAD BLACK CATS?

Are black cats lucky or unlucky? There are lots of arguments about that! But a long time ago in Europe they had rather nasty connections with witches. In America, some people believed in the magic power of the black-cat bone. Certain bones had the power to make wishes come true - or even to make the bone-owner invisible!

Nowadays, this watchful owl is thought to be a wise, harmless bird.

In days gone by, this black cat would have been in hiding at Hallowe'en!

SNAILS' TRAILS

Catch a snail on Hallowe'en night and shut it in a flat dish. In the morning, you'll see the first letter of your sweetheart written in slime!

BEASTLY BATS?

Let's finish with nice animals . . . bats. At ancient November Samhain festivals, bats used to swoop over blazing fires to guzzle all the . . . mosquitoes! Nowadays at Hallowe'en, Atlanta Zoo opens the doors to its bat-house. Would you dare go in?

What secrets will this snail reveal?

🦇 Scary stories 🦇

SIT ROUND THE FIRE and switch off the lights. Huddle close and listen to the terrible Hallowe'en tales of Jack-o'-lantern. Don't be scared - they're only stories . . . aren't they? But who was Jack?

Jack was a lad who had no fear of the devil. He strolled to a crossroads at midnight to meet him. There, they made a deal. Jack said, 'Look, you just let me have seven years full of all the fun I like. Then you can come and take me down to hell with you.'

Don't be tricked by the light! It's leading this traveller into the marshes.

At night, marshland like this sometimes glows with chemical lights known as Jack-o'- lantern.

So Jack did just as he wanted for seven whole years. But the devil didn't forget about him. He knocked on Jack's door and Jack let him in. 'Come in, come in!' said he. 'But before we set off for hell, just reach up above the door and get that old shoe for me - could you?'

The devil was happy to help. He stretched up his hand and - WHAM! Jack nailed the devil's hand to the wall. 'I'll let you go,' laughed Jack, 'But you'll have to promise not to come for me any more.' The devil promised.

When Jack finally died, no one wanted his soul. Heaven refused him - so did hell. 'Be off with you,' snarled the devil as he threw a ball of fire at Jack.

So Jack just wanders, shining with his fiery glow. But he has his fun, too. Be careful at night - don't follow his light. He likes to lead curious folk into a thick, sticky bog.

Jack-o'-lantern Hallowe'en stories came from ancient Ireland and were taken to America many years ago. There, as with many customs, they were enriched by African traditions. Some of the stories tell the fate of people who follow the eerie dancing light that flickers over misty marshes. The light is known as Jack-o'-lantern.

Let's celebrate!

JOIN IN THE HALLOWE'EN FUN! Try making some orange Hallowe'en lanterns and a Hallowe'en animal mobile.

MAKING A HALLOWE'EN LANTERN

These are for a spooky night-time party out of doors. You should never light these (or anything else!) inside. When they're made, place them on stones or sand, well away from anything that can burn. As with fireworks, always keep a bucket of water handy.

You will need:
1 large, soft oranges
2 a knife – not too sharp
3 safe scissors
4 a night-light or small candle

All you need to do is:
1 Cut the orange into two pieces. Make the top larger than the bottom.
2 Scoop out the insides – and eat them or make them into juice!
3 Cut a big hole in the top of the larger piece of orange. Then cut out eyes, a nose and the top half of the mouth.
4 Cut out the mouth in the bottom half of the orange.
5 Put your night-light in the bottom half. Ask an adult to light it and put on the top half of the orange.

28

MAKING A HALLOWE'EN MOBILE

You will need:

1 coloured card – or you can paint white card in different colours
2 two sticks of the same length
3 thread – such as fishing tackle or strong cotton
4 safe scissors
5 a thin knitting needle

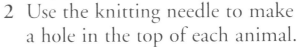

All you need to do is:

1 Cut your Hallowe'en animal shapes. You could trace round pictures in a magazine or book to help you.
2 Use the knitting needle to make a hole in the top of each animal.
3 Thread different lengths of fishing tackle or cotton through the holes. Tie the thread round the hole.
4 Cross the sticks over and wind thread round and round the middle to tie the sticks together. Make a tight knot to finish. Tie a loop to hang up your mobile.
5 Now tie the animals to the sticks, wherever you want them. Move the animals up and down the sticks until the mobile balances.

Glossary

ancestors family members of long ago
ancient something that is very old
celebrate to show that a certain day or event is special
celebrations ways of celebrating a special day, such as parades or parties
demons wicked spirits
saint a good person, thought to be especially holy after they have died
soul the human spirit - the part that is left when the body dies
spirits beings that you can't see - a bit like ghosts
temple a place of worship
tradition a custom, an old way of doing something

Index